BIRDS
OF
CANADA

CLB 2032

©1988 Colour Library Books Ltd., Godalming, Surrey, England.
All rights reserved.
This edition published 1991 by Bramley Books.
Colour separations by Hong Kong Graphic Arts Ltd., Hong Kong.
Printed and bound by Leefung Asco Printers Ltd., Hong Kong.
Photographs page 20 bottom, 21, 22, 23, 58, 59, 72, 73, 86, 87, 96, 97, 106,
    107, 110, 111, 124, 125, 132, 133, 140-145, 152-157 by Tom Hall.
All other photography © 1988 Bruce Coleman Ltd., Uxbridge, Middlesex, England.
ISBN 0 86283 639 5

BIRDS
OF
CANADA

Frank Shaw

BRAMLEY BOOKS

Looking down from a satellite in orbit over the north pole, the icecap can be seen extending outwards in all directions. In winter, the whiteness creeps close to the horizon; in summer, land appears as mountain tops and islands. This icecap is actually frozen sea, and the nearest actual land is the northernmost part of the Canadian archipelago and Greenland.

At 83°10' north, Cape Columbia on Ellesmere Island is only marginally further from the pole than Kap Morris Jesup in Greenland. Both lie much further north than any point in the Old World, and that includes Svalbard and the islands of Siberia. In the south, Windsor in Ontario lies on the same latitude as Bordeaux in France, though sadly Canada's most southerly point does not produce the fine red vintages of the world's greatest wine-growing region.

In the east, St. John's in Newfoundland is considerably nearer Ireland than it is to Vancouver, and there are no less than six different time zones between Goose Bay in Labrador and Mackenzie in the Yukon. Not surprisingly, Canada offers a huge range of climates, vegetation and landscapes to both man and wildlife, yet in this whole vast area less than six hundred different birds have ever been recorded, compared with over 2000 species in Columbia, and 1700 in Venezuela.

Ornithologically, however, Canada is no richer and no poorer than any other temperate and Arctic landmass; there are simply fewer species in these latitudes than there are in the tropics. In this respect, Canada can be compared with northern Europe, with most of the Soviet Union and with Alaska. Despite the differences in longitude, all of these areas have much in common and are home to remarkably similar types of birds. There are grouse and cranes, eagles and buteos, ducks and geese, waders and gulls that, if not actually identical, at least exhibit shared characteristics. Some have evolved from common ancestors, some are separated only at subspecific level and some are actually the same. Many of the latter have a complete circumpolar distribution and the birder in Canada can enjoy the same sights and sounds as his (or her) counterpart in the Soviet Union and northern Europe.

Returning to our polar viewpoint and looking down on the planet once more we can see the ice cap gradually giving way to tundra, then to the dwarf vegetation of the taiga zone. This, in turn, gives way to the great coniferous forests that still clothe much of the Arctic. Canada is the only country in the world where all of the zones are of easy and open access to birders. Alaska and northern Scandinavia are accessible to a more limited extent, while the whole of the Soviet Arctic is, at best, difficult of access and, at worst, completely out of bounds. Put simply, if you want to see arctic birds, there is no finer place than Canada.

Though Canada has a huge coastline, the land is for the most part surrounded by cold seas that have little insulating effect upon it. Britain, Iceland and Norway, for example, lie on similar latitudes to Newfoundland, Great Bear Lake and Baffin Island, but they are warmed by the Gulf Stream and have less severe winters as a result. The cold surrounding waters, along with the vast inland mass of Canada, give it a typically continental type of climate, with fierce winters, when temperatures hover at freezing point and below for weeks at a time, and extensive snowfall. Summers, by contrast, are warm and, in the south, even hot.

Not surprisingly, much of Canada's wildlife is seasonal, and none more so than birds. Caribou make long migrations from the summer tundra to the shelter of the great forests in winter. Bears hibernate and vegetation dies back, shedding its leaves to protect it from the killing effects of long periods of sub-zero temperatures. Birds are, however, the most mobile of all animals and capable of the most prodigious journeys. Some can fly from one end of the world to the other in a matter of a few brief weeks and do so twice each year to enjoy twelve months of summer. Such long-distance migrants are, not surprisingly, well represented among the Canadian avifauna.

But why do birds make these long and dangerous migrations, when they could remain nearer the equator and enjoy year-round warmth and sunshine? Such a simple question deserves a simple answer. Like the mountaineer who is asked why he climbs the highest peaks, the answer is 'because it is there'. Birds migrate because the Arctic, with its wealth of summer food, is there! It is a generalization to invent a neat rule that if there is a source of food then some animal will have adapted a way to take advantage of it.

The Arctic teems with life in summer, as any fisherman or hunter will tell you. In its most obvious form there are billions of mosquitoes that spend their winters in egg or larval form and in summer descend upon walkers and campers with unashamed delight and ferocity. But they are just the most obvious of a host of different water-dependent insects that have evolved a lifestyle that enables them to exploit the Arctic wilderness. The first impression gained by any visitor to the north is of the huge extent of water in summer. For the birds of Canada, the wealth of summer food is worth the hazards of migration.

Canada is, however, considerably more than the most convenient place in the world to bird the Arctic. The southern border with the United States runs artificially along the 49th parallel from British Columbia to Manitoba. Only then does it follow a more reasonable geographic path through the chain of the Great Lakes and along the St. Lawrence River until it cuts eastward on the 45th parallel to the watershed and the coast near Saint John, New Brunswick. This 'natural' section of the border that follows a central path along the Great Lakes is particularly important, not only to the Canadian population and Canadian ornithology, but to the ornithology of the whole of North America. The lakes are vast inland seas and form a considerable barrier to birds migrating north and south through the centre of the continent. The land bridges offer a waterless route to soaring birds, unable or unwilling to cross large bodies of water. But the propensity of other birds to land at the nearest coastline has turned two major promontories into major staging posts on the Canadian shore. Point Pelee, on Lake Ontario, and Long Point, on Lake Erie, have both become major bird observatories, with international reputations. Both attract visitors from all over the world to watch the fall-out of small migrants on their journeys.

In the far west, the Alaskan Purchase gave the United States sovereignty over the whole of that vast land as well as southwards along the Pacific panhandle as far as Prince Rupert. Here, in the Yukon, lie the beginnings of that chain of mountains that extends southwards through Canada and the western United States as far as Mexico. The Rockies are not only spectacularly beautiful and rich in bird life, they also present a considerable barrier to birds moving east to west. As a result, migrational pathways tend to run north to south, or even predominantly eastwards.

Canada is a highly variable land, a land that extends over huge distances from east to west, and includes the high arctic wastes of the archipelago, as well as the milder climes of southern Ontario. It is a land in which a great variety of birds can find a niche and into which migrants pour for the long, long days of a remarkably short summer. Among the most important, as well as the most spectacular, of these are the wildfowl, the swans, geese and duck.

The Arctic Wastes
No one can say how many wild geese breed in Canada. In autumn, vast skeins pass southward from their northern breeding grounds onward to their wintering grounds to the south. By far the most widespread is the Canada goose, which breeds from coast to coast across the country, northwards as far as southern Baffin and Victoria islands and southward into the United States. Almost every pot hole, pond and lake holds breeding pairs of these elegant birds. Though they vary both in size and colour and have, as a result, been divided into several distinct subspecies, it is probably best to regard them all as members of one superspecies. The smallest western subspecies have a distinctive cackling call and are often referred to as 'cackling geese', but they too are best regarded as no more than a distinctive race.

Most Canadians live in the south of the country and see these birds only on migration. They are taken alternately as a sign of spring and a sign of the approaching winter. In both seasons they fly in family flocks, for unlike many other birds, geese do not have an inbuilt migration map and young birds are dependent on their parents to lead them along the way on their first journey south and the first spring return to their breeding grounds. In other parts of the world, notably Britain, where these attractive birds have been introduced, this migration pattern has been lost and the birds make only local movements to feed and to gather at safe communal moulting grounds. This lack of high flying wild birds has resulted in an almost complete dismissal of their sporting qualities by wildfowlers. They are, thus, tame and confiding at park ponds and are increasing dramatically as a result. In parts of Britain they are already regarded as a pest.

The same cannot be said in Canada. Here, they are one of the primary quarries of the fall shooting season and many are killed every year as they pass through on their way south. In the United States, too, Canada geese are heavily hunted throughout the winter months. Yet despite the heavy toll taken annually, there is no apparent decrease in their numbers.

Given any luck, pairs remain together for life, making their journeys across the continent with successive broods of young. If and when one member dies, the survivor will take another mate, but will then remain faithful to the new partner until death. Such a strong pair bond is essential if the new season's youngsters are to be safely taught the lessons of route finding and the location of winter quarters.

The other abundant goose is the snow goose, which comes in two colour phases: white and blue. At one time these were regarded as separate species, but now only the diminutive Ross's goose is regarded as distinct. Blue phase birds are more common in the east than the west on their breeding range, but only white birds occur east of Quebec on migration. These are high arctic birds that breed in loose colonies among the tundra. They are most abundant among the archipelago, but have southern strongholds around the shores of Hudson Bay, notably at Churchill. This is the most accessible area in the world where these bold black and white geese can be seen, and it is here that most of the television movies of these birds on their breeding grounds are made. At the end of the summer they move southward in huge flocks across the prairies and onwards along the Mississippi flyway to winter along the Gulf coast of the United States. The more westerly populations head for California and the west coast of Mexico, while the larger birds of Baffin Island head for Cap Tourmente in Quebec, before passing southward to the Atlantic coast. Ross's goose has only a few major colonies among the western arctic islands and flies along a narrow corridor through Alberta and British Columbia to winter in California.

If geese are the most spectacular of these northern migrants, then the ducks must be among the most numerous. For generations the pot hole country of the prairies has been regarded as the great breeding ground of untold numbers of duck. Mallard, pintail, wigeon, blue-winged and green-winged teal breed here in their thousands, along with redhead, canvasback, ring-necked duck and lesser scaup. All fly southwards at the end of the season to be greeted by American hunters who take an enormous toll on their numbers. American money, via Ducks Unlimited, has been used to safeguard these breeding grounds, but the numbers of several species have shown a continuing decline in recent years, a decline that can only be attributed to over hunting.

Many of the arctic duck are more fortunate, spending only their summers on land and the rest of the year at sea. The fact that they are not regarded as 'game' by hunters is doubtless due more to their culinary quality than their difficulty to hit. Two species of eider, three species of scoter, plus oldsquaw, common and red-breasted mergansers are all generally ignored by sportsmen.

If breeding wildfowl are the major attraction of the north of Canada, then the shorebirds or waders run them a close second. The wealth of species is staggering and can be compared only with Alaska and northern Siberia. For many of these birds Canada represents their major breeding grounds, yet to get any idea of the numbers involved we must count them on migration or in winter, when they gather on marsh and estuary thousands of miles to the south. In most cases this has, as yet, proved impossible and we can only guess at the numbers of birds involved. The semi-palmated sandpiper is probably the most abundant shorebird of the New World, yet virtually the whole world population nests in northern Canada. It has the centre of its range in the Northwest Territories, but extends southward around the shores of Hudson Bay to the coasts of Labrador and northwards into north and west Alaska. The whole population moves south-eastward through Canada, where it is often abundant around the Great Lakes and in Newfoundland. This easterly route is used by many high arctic waders that spend their winter in South America, for it lies on the great circle route that offers the shortest distance between two points on the earth's surface. Many shorebirds, including the semi-palmated sandpiper, thus fly far out over the Atlantic every autumn and are prone to be caught up in westerly gales and swept off course to Europe. Were it not so easily confused with the European little stint, perhaps this would prove the most regular North American bird to cross the Atlantic. As it is this dubious distinction rests with the pectoral sandpiper, which occupies a similar breeding and wintering range.

Another shorebird that formerly used the same autumn route over the Atlantic was the Eskimo curlew. Prior to 1880 this small version of the Whimbrel descended in vast autumn flocks on the coasts of Labrador from its breeding grounds in the north-west. It was greeted by a fusilade of shot that was equalled only by that which was offered to the now extinct passenger pigeon across the border to the south. Earlier, the Eskimo curlew too had, on several occasions, managed a transatlantic journey, only to be shot by some British enthusiast. Today there are only a scattering of records from the Gulf Coast of Texas in spring. No doubt this bird still breeds in Canada, but it will be a fortunate birder that finds it doing so.

American golden plover, black-bellied plover, semi-palmated plover, whimbrel, Hudsonian godwit, upland sandpiper, buff-breasted sandpiper, solitary sandpiper, spotted sandpiper, greater and lesser yellowlegs, stilt sandpiper, short-billed dowitcher, ruddy turnstone, purple sandpiper, knot, dunlin, sanderling, the peeps, and two species of phalaropes all make this length-of-the-continent migration to take advantage of the wealth of summer food and nesting security offered by the Arctic. For most Canadians they are only passage migrants, birds that pass through twice each year.

Wildfowl and waders share their arctic home with a variety of other species, almost all of which are also migrants unable to sustain life through the winter freeze-up. Some are similarly long distance migrants, while others move only as far as is necessary to find suitable hunting conditions. The jaegers and terns are good examples of other long-distance migrants that leave the country completely, while many of the arctic breeding birds of prey move southwards only as far as the forest zone of Canada.

By far the most common jaeger is the parasitic, which spends its summer hunting lemmings among the tundra. Like the other species, the pomarine and long-tailed jaegers, it migrates over the sea and along the coasts and is only rarely found in the interior. For most Canadians these high arctic birds can be seen only on their breeding grounds, or in spring and autumn when they pass along both east and west coasts. Newfoundland, Labrador and Nova Scotia offer splendid sea-watching opportunities for these and other pelagic birds, but large numbers are also found along the Pacific coast and between Vancouver and Vancouver Island. In the autumn they are often seen following the flocks of terns moving southwards and, outside the breeding season, they are predominantly pirates. Swift, almost falcon-like fliers, jaegers select and chase their victim with remarkable agility and tenacity. Eventually, the hapless tern drops its hard-won meal, which the jaeger grabs before it reaches the water. All along their long journeys to the southern oceans, the terns have these pirates for company.

The terns themselves are, of course, the longest distance migrants of all. Arctic terns nest throughout the tundra zone, extending as far north as the ice-free coasts of northern Ellesmere Island, only a few hundred miles from the pole itself. They also nest southward along the coasts of Nova Scotia and New Brunswick. At the end of the breeding season they move southward along the coasts, through Atlantic and Pacific to the Antarctic Ocean, a distance of 11,000 miles, in some cases. Strange as it may seem, birds that breed in north-eastern Canada head straight out across the Atlantic to make a landfall along the coasts of Europe, before heading south to Africa. On arrival off the coasts of the Antarctic they then spread out and may even reach Australia, a prodigious journey for such a lightweight bird. These are indeed truly globe-spanners, the most travelled animals on earth.

Jaegers are not the only predators that find a home in the lushness of the arctic summer. Wolf, polar and grizzly bears, arctic fox and the birds of prey are also present to take advantage of the wealth of food available. But, while the mammals are limited in how far they can move when winter sets in, the rapacious birds simply open their wings and sail southwards to milder climes. Even among this group of birds there are, however, marked differences. The peregrine falcon breeds in the Arctic but migrates southward, leaving Canada almost completely. Sadly, this magnificent bird has been decimated in numbers since the 1950s pesticide mania, and is only slowly regaining its former status. The gyrfalcon, in contrast, breeds as far north as ice-free land extends, but moves southward only to the boreal zone of the conifer forests. Most birds thus remain within Canadian borders, though occasionally these great white birds move southwards into the northern United States. Occasionally, birds that breed in Greenland make a transatlantic journey to Europe where, of course, they attract birders in their hundreds. There is no reason to suppose that the occasional Canadian bird does not make a similar journey.

Two quite distinct birds of prey that occupy similar breeding ranges in the Arctic have quite different migratory habits. Both are small mammal specialists, but while the rough-legged hawk leaves its range to winter in southern Canada and across the border in the United States, the snowy owl usually just moves to the boreal zone. Even in the harshest of winters, this great white predator is but a rare visitor to the northern United States, and many birds remain on their breeding grounds despite the covering of ice. Though they mostly move from the zone of complete winter darkness, they are probably the most northerly wintering birds in the world. With a dense covering of insulating feathers and completely feathered legs and feet, they inhabit bleak, open countryside where they hunt, unlike most other owls, during the hours of daylight. About every four or five years they irrupt southwards, often in large numbers. These periodic movements are triggered off by the movement southward of their staple diet, the lemming. At such times they may be quite common in southern Canada and reach well southward into the United States.

The Great Conifer Forests

Unlike the snowy owl, most other owls are nocturnal and resident. They generally inhabit woodland, and the majority are found among the huge conifer forests that cover such a large area of Canada. Indeed, the mapped distribution of several species coincides exactly with that of these trees. There is, however, no doubt that mapping where trees are found is far easier than mapping owl distributions, and most ornithologists base their distribution maps on the presence of appropriate habitat, rather than proven presence of the birds. Hawk owl, boreal owl and great gray owl show a total dependence on the boreal zone, though they are not the only species to be found there. Others, such as the great horned owl, long-eared owl, boreal owl and saw-whet owl are all widespread among the conifers, but also occupy other woodland habitats to the south. Others still, like the tiny flammulated and pygmy owls, are more mountain based.

All in all the forests of northern Canada are among the richest owl habitats in the world, yet these birds are remarkably difficult to see elsewhere. Several actually enjoy a circumpolar distribution and are thus also found in the great forests that extend across Eurasia from Scandinavia to Kamchatka. Yet these regions are largely out of bounds to birders and, while Europeans scour the forests of northern Sweden and Finland for hawk, great gray, pygmy and boreal owls, they would be much better advised to try Canada. Even so, these are never easy birds to locate.

Most owls start to breed early in the new year, when ice and snow still covers the ground and daytime temperatures remain persistently below freezing. At this time they can be located by their calls and traced back to their nests and young. The visitor without local contacts will then see the prominently perched hawk owl, but will otherwise be fortunate to find another species, let alone the complete set.

Another group of birds that finds a natural home among the forests is the grouse. Though three species, the ptarmigans, are birds of tundra and mountain, the most spectacular members of this family are inhabitants of conifer forests and clearings.

The spruce grouse, ruffed grouse and sharp-tailed grouse are splendid birds, with elaborate nuptial plumages and spectacular displays. The similar, but larger, blue grouse is more a bird of mountainous deciduous woodland, though it too resorts to conifers in winter.

All of these birds are resident within the boreal zone, though each has a favoured summer niche. The ruffed grouse, for example, haunts forest clearings and edges, particularly where birch scrub is the dominant vegetation; indeed, Canadian sportsmen usually refer to it as the birch grouse. It has its counterparts in the Old World, where both the hazel grouse and Sewerzow's grouse occupy similar niches and were once placed within the same genus.

The ruffed grouse is highly prized by hunters, for not only is it delicious to eat, but it is generally regarded as quarry for only the most excellent of shots. When disturbed, it takes to the air with a great clattering of wings like a pheasant, and apparently puts the trunks of trees between itself and the hunter quite deliberately. True or not, it is a very special bird. In the forests of early spring its sounds are both evocative and unique. Starting with a series of deep thuds, the sound rapidly develops into a whining that lasts upwards of ten seconds. A close approach reveals the male standing on a specially-chosen fallen log, with an extended and puffed up black ruff surrounding its head. Though this is the 'ruff' from which it takes its name, the turkey-like fanned tail is far more obvious. Shaded in tones of rufous-brown, it is finely barred and broadly tipped with black and white. The perfect symmetry is startlingly beautiful, but this is not the end of the ruffed grouse mystery.

Lowering its tail, it slowly starts to beat its

wings to produce the dull thumping sound. Gradually the wings are beaten faster and faster until the air vibrates and too close an approach will actually hurt the human eardrum. At the end of what is actually one of the very few avian instrumental performances, the cock ruffed grouse struts up and down his log in a most comical way.

Though this is one of the most spectacular, all of the grouse in one way or another, produce a display of sound and plumage designed to attract a mate. Females are similar, but much duller than the males and, once mated, take sole responsibility for the nest, incubation and care of the young. Being ground nesters they are heavily camouflaged and sit tightly, even when danger threatens. Female grouse make excellent mothers, leading the chicks from the nest, brooding them during the night and teaching them to feed themselves. If threatened, the chicks crouch stock still on the ground, while the female performs an elaborate act of injury-feigning designed to draw the would-be predator from her brood.

One would expect these great northern forests to be full of woodpeckers, but this is not the case. Most woodpeckers avoid stands of pure conifer, preferring instead either deciduous woodland, or mixed conifer-deciduous forests. Several prefer more open country, and almost all create their nests either in dead trees or living deciduous ones. The trouble with conifers is that when cut or damaged they bleed a sticky resin that quickly coats birds' feathers and is difficult, if not impossible, to remove. Most species thus avoid conifers for nesting, though they are quite happy to forage for food among them, and may even prefer conifers for that purpose.

Woodpeckers are highly adapted to an arboreal lifestyle. They have strong legs and feet, with the toes equipped with sharp 'climbing-iron' claws. Most have four toes, two pointing forward and two back, but a few have only three toes. They have stiff shafts to the tail feathers that provide extra support, and sharp, strong, chisel-like bills capable of hacking at bark and the living tree to reach the wood-boring insects and their larvae that form the birds' staple diet. They also have specially strengthened skulls to withstand the constant pounding without damaging the brain, and extremely long tongues to extract their food from its long, protective galleries.

Typical boreal zone woodpeckers include the yellow-shafted flicker, which prefers open areas, often feeds on the ground and nests readily enough in telegraph poles. This bird is thus also found on the treeless prairies. The huge pileated woodpecker avoids the prairies, but is found throughout the boreal forests, especially where there are dead trees in which to nest. It also nests in living deciduous trees and occasionally in living conifers. The yellow-bellied sapsucker prefers deciduous forests, or at least mixed ones.

Like the other sapsuckers, it drills a series of small holes in living trees and then later returns to 'suck" the sap and feed on the insects that have also been attracted to this liquid food. The yellow-bellied sapsucker breeds right across Canada from Vancouver to Newfoundland, though it is absent from the prairies. Like the yellow-shafted flicker, though unlike the pileated woodpecker, it is a migrant and leaves its breeding range completely in winter. The seasonal nature of its food supply precludes a year-round tenancy of the northern forests.

Both hairy and downy woodpeckers are resident in their natal forests, but are by no means confined to the boreal zone. Both breed throughout North America wherever trees are found, the larger hairy woodpecker extending southwards into Mexico. Both species are found in deciduous or mixed forests, but the downy woodpecker is generally more widespread away from forests and includes orchards, farms, city parks and bushy country among the areas it will inhabit. While the larger hairy woodpecker is quite capable of excavating a nest hole in a living tree, its smaller cousin prefers dead trees, or dead limbs and branches.

Two distinct species of three-toed woodpeckers are also found in the boreal zone and both are, if anything, better adapted to a life among the conifers than any other species. Their ranges are remarkably similar, but while the northern three-toed is quite common in western forests and rare in the east, the black-backed three-toed is rare throughout its range. Both excavate their nests holes in conifers (though not invariably) and for preference choose dead trees. They are, however, both quite capable of nesting in living trees. The differences between the species is slight, the northern having a black and white ladder-like pattern on the back.

Though many small birds find a home among the boreal forests, few are actually confined to this zone. Perhaps because they need smaller territories, these birds may find suitable habitats in small pockets throughout North America. Even among those that are found only in this zone, not all are confined to conifers. The most obvious examples of birds that actually need conifers are the crossbills, two species of which breed in Canada. But while the red or common crossbill extends from the northern forests southwards through the similar forests of the Rocky Mountains as far as the Mexican border, the distribution of the white-winged crossbill coincides almost exactly with that of the spruce, pine and larch of the boreal zone.

Similarly, both kinglets are 'conifer birds' that extend southwards into the United States in the mountain regions. These tiny birds, among Canada's smallest, flit and hover among the outer branches of conifers picking insects and larvae from among the needles. If anything, the gold-crowned is more conifer orientated than the ruby-crowned and invariably builds its nest suspended at the very tip of a high twig, where squirrels are unable to gain access. These are both confiding little birds that frequently allow a close approach as they feed. Both, despite their size, are long-distance migrants that in autumn move southwards through the more populated parts of the country to winter in the United States. Though both can be found in the same areas in winter, the ruby-crowned travels considerably further, reaching well into Mexico.

Another pair of species inhabits the boreal zone – the two waxwings. But, while the Bohemian waxwing is more or less closely associated with conifers, the cedar waxwing is more catholic in its choice of habitats. It does not exactly shun conifers, but is quite capable of doing without them. In fact, it occupies a very wide variety of vegetated areas, including open woodland, bushes and shrubs around farmsteads, brush country along streams and around lakes and marshes, indeed almost anywhere that suitable food berries can be found. The Bohemian waxwing, too, feeds on berries but, in summer at least, is always somewhere near conifers. This species is also found in the Old World where, as in Canada, it thrills birders south of its usual range by irrupting periodically. Such irruptions may bring it to the Great Lakes region, hundreds of miles east of its normal range, as well as south as far as California. These irruptions, typical of so many northern breeding species, may be triggered by a poor berry harvest, but can ultimately be regarded as caused by a previous very successful breeding season leading to extremely high

population levels. As with the lemming, such irruptions can be regarded as a simple mechanism to keep the population at levels that the habitat, and especially the winter food, can adequately sustain.

Chickadees are relatively common among the conifers, but are represented by only two species. The black-capped is a widespread and common bird found throughout most of temperate North America. It takes readily to nest boxes and comes to bird feeding stations in good numbers. It is the typical chickadee. The boreal chickadee, as its name implies, is a pure bird of the boreal zone. It does just cross the border into the United States, but is predominantly a Canadian bird. In the east it comes as far south as the great forests, but is absent from the populated areas of southern Ontario. In the north it goes as far as the limit of conifer woodland.

In late summer both species may associate with red-breasted nuthatches and brown creepers, which are summer visitors to conifer forests. Both of these tree climbing birds extend through the Rockies, but both abandon the northern forests in winter, moving southward to almost every part of the United States.

No less than thirteen of the eighteen species of thrushes that breed in North America can be found within the borders of Canada. Of these, only the American robin is widely spread throughout the continent and, though it does occur in the boreal zone, it is much less of a woodland bird than several other species of thrush. For preference it inhabits clearings and woodland margins, but is also found in gardens, in parks and around buildings. To Canada it is a summer visitor, though some do overwinter in southern Ontario and around Vancouver. All three boreal zone thrushes – species that are more or less associated with conifers – are long distance migrants that make long migrations to the United States or leave North America completely. Of the latter, the gray-checked and Swainson's thrushes are almost completely confined to conifers. The gray-checked breeds from Alaska right across the northern edge of the forests to Labrador and Newfoundland. This association with the treeline inhibits its breeding south of St. James Bay, save in the 'sea-bleak' area of Nova Scotia. For most Canadians it is no more than a bird of passage, for it winters in Peru and northern Brazil.

Though Swainson's thrush does overlap with

the gray-checked, it has a generally more southerly distribution and is frequently found where deciduous and coniferous trees meet and are mixed together. It also extends through such forests in the Rockies as far south as California. Both species are replaced to the south by the common and much better known veery.

Of all the birds of the forest zone, none have a greater appeal than the warblers. Forty-two species occur in Canada, compared with some fifty-seven in North America as a whole. Often referred to as 'wood warblers', this family is exclusively found in the New World, though their name derives from a somewhat similar group found in Europe. American birds do not, however, actually 'warble'. Just occasionally, one of these dainty migrants will make the transatlantic crossing to be identified in Europe. Most do so in October and arrive in Britain's Isles of Scilly. Strangely enough, European birders seem less daunted by the possibility of identifying a North American warbler than Americans are of identifying most of their European counterparts. Nevertheless, fall warblers, when the males lack their distinctive plumage of spring, should be treated with great respect and identified with the greatest of care.

Of Canada's forty-two species, comparatively few are confined to, or even show a preference for, conifers. Most, at best, inhabit mixed woods, and a glance at a distribution map showing the orange-crowned warbler, for example, as breeding throughout the boreal zone, hides the fact that this bird is found in deciduous woods and in the deciduous parts of mixed woods. Similarly, the Parula warbler does not mind whether it inhabits deciduous or coniferous forests, just as long as the lichen old man's beard can be found there.

More certain to be found among conifers are the Tennessee warbler, though it is also found in mixed woodland, the magnolia warbler, though this bird prefers its conifers young or stunted, and the Cape May warbler, which is widespread in the boreal zone of Canada, but decidedly local south of the border as far as Cape May, where it is best known as a migrant.

Yellow-rumped, black-throated green, Blackburnian, bay-breasted, Connecticut and blackpoll warblers all breed among conifers, though only the latter has a really positive association. At best, the others will breed among conifers, but are just as happy in mixed forests, or in pure deciduous stands. All

of the other warblers, and there are many of them, that breed in the boreal zone frequent scrub, marshside vegetation, or seek out the purely deciduous areas within these great forests. The blackpoll warbler, however, has a quite definite connection with spruce and mostly builds its nest among the lower branches of this tree. It breeds from Alaska along the northern edge of the conifer zone as far as Newfoundland, but with a few southern outposts in Nova Scotia. The whole population migrates south-eastward (it is decidedly scarce on the west coast of Texas for example) to winter from Peru and western Brazil to Chile. Here, then, is another example of great circle route migration that has in turn led to transatlantic vagrancy. Among the spruce forests of northern Canada, the song of the blackpoll warbler is a common sound of summer.

One further bird of the northern forests deserves a mention. The pine grosbeak is somewhat misnamed, for it favours spruce and fir forests in summer and is locally common in many areas. It breeds from the Pacific to the Atlantic and throughout the boreal zone of Eurasia. Its stubby, but powerful, bill is perfectly adapted to feeding on berries and buds. Though resident over much of its range, it leaves the central part of its Canadian range to winter over much of the northern and western United States. As with the crossbills, it sometimes irrupts into areas where it is otherwise unknown.

The Rocky Mountains

If we have spent an undue amount of time (and space) on the arctic tundra and the boreal forests rather than the other life zones of Canada, this is easily excused because of their uniqueness. Such huge forests can otherwise be found only behind the boundaries of the Soviet Union where, as we have already seen, they are mostly out of bounds to foreign birders.

In the Rockies we find one of the world's great mountain chains, with peaks soaring into a land of permanent ice and snow – a land where glaciers cut deep 'U'-shaped valleys into the landscape and create deltas with their summer melt. As with mountains elsewhere, climate varies enormously with altitude, and thus within a few miles one may travel from the tundra-like high tops, through the boreal zone with its covering of conifers, to gentle meadows where shirt-sleeves are the order of summer days. Thus it is that a wide variety of birds can be found among the mountains. Several species, more typical of the tundra, extend southwards, finding, at altitude, similar conditions to those prevailing at high latitude. Among the ducks, both Barrow's goldeneye and harlequin breed throughout the Rockies to the American border and beyond. Birds of prey such as goshawk, golden eagle and osprey do the same, and one could cite other examples among various groups of Canadian birds.

There are, however, some birds that seem better adapted to mountain life than to the tundra, even though they are found in both habitats; and a few that are actually exclusive to the mountains. Both willow and rock ptarmigan are found among the bare mountain tops and screes, and both have highly cryptic plumages to protect them from predators at all times of the year. Both seem more naturally at home in the mountains, where a simple vertical migration, covering at most only a few miles, protects them from the most severe conditions. The white-tailed ptarmigan, in contrast, has an almost complete mountain-based distribution and is all but confined to the Rockies. The other species are both more widespread, with completely circumpolar distributions. Among the owls, too, there is a southward extension from the boreal zone through the conifer forests of the mountains. Great gray and pygmy owls are cases in point. Both black and Vaux's swifts are mountain birds: the former nesting among cliffs and buttresses, the latter among forests. Three of the four hummingbirds that occur in Canada are found in the west among the Rockies, though only the calliope can be truly regarded as a mountain bird. That such diminutive birds should be found in Canada at all is remarkable, but the rufous hummingbird actually penetrates beyond the Canadian borders to the Alaskan panhandle.

All of the swallows once nested naturally in cliffs and caves, or along river banks. Most have benefited from human activity and have been able to spread across open countryside by taking to our buildings, sand pits and even to specially erected nesting boxes. Several species still breed in natural conditions among the Rockies, but the violet-green swallow is the most tenacious natural nester, often building at great heights among the cliffs.

Of the jays, several are predominantly birds of the conifer forests, but while the gray jay extends eastward in the boreal zone and southward through the mountains, Steller's jay has made no such colonization of the north. This attractive bird is confined to western mountain forests and is resident from southern Alaska to Mexico. It builds its nest in a conifer and is particularly fond of Douglas fir. Similarly, the mountain chickadee is confined to conifers in the Rockies. This attractive little bird, marked by a black cap and black eyestripe, nests mainly in old woodpecker holes, but will also take to nest boxes where they are made available. One of the strangest members of this family is the chestnut-backed chickadee, which is confined to the conifer forests of the western Rockies from the Alaskan panhandle, through British Columbia southwards to California. Over this range it is quite a common resident, but it is totally unknown away from its native forests.

Though North America abounds with streams and rivers, the American dipper is strangely confined to the Rockies. Here it finds a home among the fast running torrents, where streams tumble among boulders carving steep banks under which it can nest. It will also take readily to ledges beneath bridges and even the cliffs behind waterfalls. It can swim well and is capable of walking along the beds of streams and of 'flying' under water. The legs are strong, for gripping slippery rocks, and it has a special oil gland, like that of a duck, which is used to waterproof its feathers.

Mountains are generally well endowed with seed-eating birds and, indeed, many species can be found among the Rockies. They do, however, include two high altitude species that are real mountain specialists. The golden-crowned sparrow is a summer visitor to the Canadian Rockies that finds its niche near the timberline. The gray-crowned rosy finch ventures even higher, and is seldom found below 7,000 feet in summer. It regularly nests among the snow fields and glaciers, building its bulky nest in rock crevices, or even among the rock debris of the mountain-tops themselves.

The Great Plains

The Canadian prairies of Alberta and Saskatchewan have been converted from natural grassy plains to one of the most productive cereal growing areas of the world. Instead of wild grasses offering food to a variety of bird species, we now have a monoculture, mainly of wheat, stretching for hundreds of miles virtually without a break. There are, of course, homesteads and their associated wind-breaks of planted trees. There are ponds and marshes, though many have been drained and filled in the name of agricultural efficiency. There are towns and cities with introduced vegetation and huge storage silos that offer artificial cliffs where none existed before. All of these man-made changes have enabled birds that were formerly unknown on the prairies to find man-made riches to exploit. But, overall, the native birds of the plains have declined.

Of the birds of prey, those dependent on trees, such as the goshawk and sharp-shinned hawk are either absent, or highly localised in distribution. In contrast, Swainson's hawk, which is a bird that prefers the wide open spaces with only the odd tree in which to rest, finds its Canadian stronghold on the prairies. Not surprisingly, it often uses the same nest year after year. The closely related ferruginous hawk, now sadly declining in numbers, is also a plains-loving species, though it frequently nests among river banks and hillsides. Two species of falcon are also prairie birds. The prairie falcon, as its name implies, is a grassland species that requires only the old nest of another bird, a cliff ledge, or even just a rocky outcrop on which to nest, while the sparrowhawk, or American kestrel, breeds right across Canada and utilises buildings, bird boxes and tree holes to exploit the wide open spaces.

Not surprisingly, woodland grouse are absent from the plains and are replaced by the greater prairie chicken. At one time the prairies were one of the major strongholds of this species and their mating calls echoed across the grasslands. The conversion of grasslands to cereal growing undoubtedly the major cause of their decline, a decline that highly mechanised farming techniques did nothing to help. Hunters often confuse this species with the more abundant sharp-tailed grouse, but shooting alone would not have reduced the population so drastically. The prairie chicken is a victim of change and progress. It was found in Alberta, where the last record was of one at Medicine Hat in 1940. In Saskatchewan it held on longer, but only two were seen in 1959 and only one the following year. A similar story can be told of Manitoba. Today the prairie chicken breeds only in southern Ontario, hundreds of miles from the prairies for which it was named. The related sage grouse also breeds on the prairies, though it is confined to the southernmost part of the Alberta-Saskatchewan border, where the sagebrush country offers it a home. It too is declining.

Though several shorebirds can be found among the prairies, they mostly breed at the ponds and marshes and along the river banks, and thus cannot be regarded as typical grassland birds. The killdeer, however, is a grassland bird, though it breeds right across Canada and is not confined to the prairie region. The long-billed curlew, too, is not confined to this region, though it does find its major Canadian stronghold here. Despite being equipped with a huge, probing bill, it spends its summers picking food from the surface. Upland plover, willet, marbled godwit and American avocet all have their Canadian stronghold on the prairies, though by no means all of these birds are truly grassland species. Indeed, only the upland plover is truly a plains bird.

Among the gulls, only Franklin's is a prairie bird, but like the avocet it inhabits marshes and lakes. It does, however, find most of its food on agricultural land and often forages in large flocks. The range of the strange burrowing owl in Canada is almost entirely confined to the prairies. Typically, it adopts the disused hole of a ground-dwelling mammal as its nest and lays its eggs up to ten feet underground. The spoil heap from the excavation makes an admirable lookout perch, though like the original occupant the bird quickly disappears when approached.

A glance through the distribution maps of many of the smaller Canadian birds reveals an obvious gap in the prairies. Indeed, there are so many examples that a list of such species would be boring. Instead, a few examples of birds that are prairie specialists is much more informative. Most are species that, as one would expect, spend much of their time on the ground. Sprague's pipit is, along with the Arctic and mountain-based water pipit and the rare Yukon-based yellow wagtail, the only member of this large Old World family to have colonised North America. It prefers natural grassland to plough, and extends southward across the American border. Though more widespread, the western meadowlark is similarly a bird of open prairie, though it is particularly fond of spilt and wasted grain in autumn. Like the pipit, it is a long-clawed bird with strong legs for walking. Similarly, the well named longspurs, McCowan's and chestnut-collared, are typical grassland birds that in Canada are confined to the prairies. Indeed, both species find their total world range in the great grasslands that extend north and south of the American border. Both are, however, only summer visitors, moving southward to the more arid country around the Mexican border in winter.

The Coasts

The coastlines of Canada are among the most spectacular in the world. Mostly they are rocky, with steep cliffs and a maze of offshore islands of varying size. Estuaries are few, because rivers are short in the west, drain into the Arctic seas in the north or into the giant Great Lakes – St. Lawrence system in the east. Nevertheless, huge numbers of wildfowl and shorebirds manage to find sufficient food to see them through their journeys to and from their northern breeding grounds. It is, however, with the true seabirds, birds that find nesting sites among the cliffs and stacks, that we are concerned here. Some of the greatest seabird colonies in the world can be found on Canadian shores. There are cliffs where uncounted thousands of birds nest cheek by jowl; islands where hole-nesting birds simply cannot be counted, and stacks simply covered with birds.

Canada is fortunate in having its two major coastlines separated by over three thousand miles of non-seabird territory. Most birds are thus confined to one or the other, and a journey across the continent from the Atlantic to the Pacific is required if a representative list of Canadian birds is to be amassed. Additionally, there are some seabirds that are confined to the northern coasts, where they remain largely inaccessible, though not out of bounds.

Although a large number of seabirds have been seen 'off' Canadian shores, this section concentrates on those that breed. It thus omits the three species of albatross that have been recorded, one reasonably regularly, off the Pacific coast, as well as the various shearwaters that have been seen both on the Pacific and Atlantic. Of the true seabirds only Leach's petrel breeds on both the Atlantic and Pacific coasts. This is a widespread bird that is found throughout the northern hemisphere. It spends its winters at sea and nests in burrows and among clefts in rocks on small, mainly uninhabited, islands. Birds that breed on the Pacific coast are slightly smaller than those that breed on the Atlantic, and have been assigned to a distant sub-species. Atlantic birds also occur in the Pacific as far as the Aleutians and must, therefore, roam the seas via Cape Horn or the Cape of Good Hope, presumably the latter.

Gannets are found only along the Atlantic coast, where there are major colonies in Newfoundland and Quebec, most notably at Bonaventure Island, where thousands of pairs of these great black and white birds nest on the sloping cliffs. The great cormorant also has its headquarters at the mouth of the St. Lawrence, but is replaced on the Pacific coast by the pelagic cormorant. These are gregarious birds that find their food by diving from the surface, usually close inshore.

Most gulls nest in the north among the archipelago, but the great black-backed is almost exclusively Atlantic and the glaucous-winged, Pacific. The former has on occasion also nested as far west as the Great Lakes. Glaucous, Iceland, Thayer's, Sabine's, ivory and Ross's gulls are all Arctic breeding species, the last being only recently discovered breeding in the New World. Black-legged kittiwakes also breed in the Arctic, but are primarily an Atlantic bird with large colonies in Newfoundland and adjacent Quebec. This species is replaced in the Pacific by the red-legged kittiwake which is, however, only a rare straggler to Canadian waters.

Among the auks, the razorbill and common murre are both found along the Atlantic coast, the latter being replaced further north by the thick-billed murre. The two can be found nesting alongside one another in north-eastern Newfoundland and along the eastern coast of Labrador. The Atlantic-based black guillemot breeds from Nova Scotia eastwards along the coast of Baffin Island to southern Melville. It is a black bird with bold white wing patches in summer. The very similar pigeon guillemot is confined to the Pacific coast and has two black bars breaking the white wing patch.

The auklets and puffins obviously evolved in the Pacific and most still have their centre of distribution in this area. Only the common puffin has colonised the Atlantic, where it now breeds on both sides of the ocean. The similar tufted puffin is purely a Pacific bird. The smaller members of this group, called auklets and murrelets, are marked by various tufts, horns and other head ornaments. All, without exception, are Pacific birds. Among the least spectacular is the marbled murrelet which, although common along the Canadian coast, remained an enigma until comparatively recently. Although clearly a seabird, its breeding behaviour was shrouded in mystery, with birds leaving the sea and flying strongly away inland during the breeding season. Only in the last decade has it finally been proved that these little black and white birds nest in broken tree tops. The Queen Charlotte Islands are the Canadian breeding centre of several of these small auks, though they are also found northwards into Alaska. Here, ancient murrelet, Cassin's auklet and rhinoceros auklet, as well as tufted puffin, all breed.

In late summer many seabirds start their long migrations southwards toward winter quarters, while others drift away from their breeding colonies in more local movements. By early autumn many coastal headlands offer really exciting birding to those prepared to spend long hours staring out to sea. Mostly these are Canadian birds, but several other species may be quite regular. Some southern ocean birds spend their winter in the north, making huge, loop-like journeys across the northern oceans. The sooty and great shearwaters are examples in the Atlantic, while pink-footed and pale-footed shearwaters occur along the Pacific coast.

More recently, birders have taken to the sea to observe these birds. Such 'pelagic trips', as they are known, are growing in popularity and adding considerably to our knowledge of the movements of many species. Even those lacking sea-legs can, however, gain great enjoyment from watching seabirds move along Canadian shores.

Epilogue

Canada is, as we have seen, a vast country of diverse landscapes, yet it has a comparatively small population concentrated mainly in the south-east. Among this population birders are naturally few, forming no larger, nor smaller a proportion of the total than in any other nation. On this small band of enthusiasts our knowledge of the Canadian avifauna depends, yet they have a far larger area to cover than most other bird-orientated nations. While it is unlikely that there are

birds new to science waiting to be discovered within its boundaries (such birds tend to be hidden away in the tropical rainforests of the southern hemisphere), there are probably birds breeding in Canada about which no one knows. The recent discovery of Ross's gull breeding exactly opposite their only other known breeding area in north central Siberia, but separated by the north pole, shows that our knowledge of this vast wilderness is far from complete. There seems little doubt that more such birds will be found in the future.

Growing expertise with the skills of identification, especially of juvenile birds in dull autumn plumages, will doubtless continue to add new birds to the Canadian list. Intensive banding programmes at, say, Cape Race in Newfoundland and in northern Queen Charlotte Island, should produce vagrants from Europe and Asia respectively. Even in the most heavily birded areas of America and Europe, new vagrant species are still being found every year. Some of these can be predicted, but others are among the most unexpected. If a bald eagle can find its way to Ireland, as one apparently did in 1987, then there must be possibilities of even Steller's sea eagle occuring in the New World.

Vagrancy and new colonizations are, of course, among the most exciting aspects of contemporary ornithology, but in Canada there is enormous potential for studies that may be relatively commonplace elsewhere. Mapping and census work might seem, in so vast a landscape, to be out of the question. But sampling techniques can be adapted to suit any circumstances, and correctly handled would produce outstanding advances in our knowledge of Canadian birds. The growth of bird-tourism in itself does no harm, but it could actually produce worthwhile results if visitors reported their observations to the appropriate state bird organisation.

Above all though, Canada offers splendid birds in a splendid wilderness. It is something that should be treasured.

Previous page: a male western tanager. The adult male is distinguished from the female by its red head, both sexes having bright yellow underparts and conspicuous double wing bars. Above: the handsome arctic loon near its nest, resplendent in its summer plumage. This loon breeds on freshwater lakes in the remote north and winters on the coast. Another water bird, the pintail (facing page top) is widespread. The male is distinguished from the female by his chocolate brown head, white neck and long, central tail feathers, the female having buff brown feathers streaked with black. Franklin's gull (facing page bottom) is a small, black-headed, red-billed gull that breeds on prairie lakes or marshes and feeds in flocks in fields.

Breeding almost throughout Canada, the Canada goose (top) varies greatly in size depending on the sub-species, but all of them show the distinctive black head and neck with the white throat and cheek patches that form a throat strap. The sexes are similar in appearance and breed adjacent to lakes, streams and marshes. Above: a female snowy owl, whose distinctive brown barring distinguishes it from the almost completely white male. In summer the snowy owl feeds on lemmings in the northern tundra, moving further south as winter approaches. The bald eagle (facing page) was once heavily hunted and also suffered from pesticide poisoning, but now, fully protected, its numbers are stabilizing. Fish form the main part of this eagle's diet, and it is most commonly found in Alaska. The adult is easily recognised by its white head and massive yellow bill.

The Canada goose (these pages) is **the** wild goose of the country. Most people see it on its spring or fall migration to and from its breeding grounds. Its nest is a depression in the ground lined with sticks and dried stems, with an inner lining of down. The young hatch out after 28 to 33 days.

Facing page: a female mallard keeps watch while her ducklings rest. A common duck, the mallard breeds mainly in western Canada and is found almost anywhere associated with freshwater ponds, lakes, marshes and floodwater, sometimes even seen on the coast in winter. The mallard feeds by upending in the water, paddling its feet to keep upright, with just its rear end visible above the surface. The orange and black bill of the female distinguishes it from similar species. Above: a fox sparrow busily feeding its young, a task assumed by both parents. This bird builds a rather bulky nest lined with wool or feathers low down in bushes or on the ground, and lays three to five eggs. It is quite common, especially in western Canada.

The colourful male wood duck (previous pages), with its glossy green head, striking red eye and red bill, is a bird of woodland lakes and streams, as its name implies. It nests, not by the water's edge, but in holes or hollows in trees, and when the young hatch they climb to the entrance and drop to the ground. Previous pages inset: a female American robin feeding its brood. A familiar bird, this robin is common throughout Canada in the summer months.

The broad-winged hawk (facing page) is one of the smaller hawks, and is found mainly in woodlands. When hunting it is usually alone, perched waiting for prey such as snakes, frogs or mice to pass below, yet large numbers of these hawks can be seen congregating for migration in the autumn. Above: a bald eagle, bill agape, uttering its squealing 'kik-kik-kik' call.

Facing page: two seven-week-old bald eagle chicks patiently await their parents' return with food. These birds will fly in another three to four weeks, but still may return to the nest for food. Yellow-bellied sapsuckers (top left), like all sapsuckers, are so named for their habit of drilling holes in trees, which they later visit to feed on both the sap and the various insects attracted to the sweet resin. They are common in deciduous woodland. A broad black-and-white-striped crown and a pinkish bill help distinguish the white-crowned sparrow from other sparrows, though some birds may have a more yellow bill (top right). They are common in woodland thickets, parks and shrubbery. Above: young ospreys nearly ready to leave the nest. Ospreys are uncommon and, as they feed only on fish, are found chiefly on the coast, or near lakes and rivers.

With short, rounded wings and a long tail, the goshawk (facing page) is ideally suited to chasing and catching prey in woodland. Flying through the trees at low level, it swoops on its prey, such as squirrels and grouse. The long, yellow legs and feet of this hawk, with their large, needle-sharp claws, are ideal for clasping and gripping prey, and the bird itself is easily identified by a pale line over its eye. Above: ospreys preparing to mate on their huge, bulky nest made of sticks and twigs. Three eggs are usually laid, and are incubated by the female. Ospreys feed exclusively on fish, which they catch by hovering over the water until suitable prey is spotted, then diving spectacularly to the water, feet first, catching the fish in their deeply-curved talons.

Above: a great horned owl, woken from its sleep during the day, a time when it is often found and mobbed by crows. Its large size and conspicuous ear tufts identify this particular owl, which inhabits both deciduous and coniferous woodland, city parks and river valleys, and hunts rabbits, skunks, ducks and grouse, as well as rats and mice. Its call is a loud, deep hoot, usually uttered three or five times. The much smaller screech owl (facing page) also has 'ears', but is only about a third of the size of the great horned owl. The screech owl is found in a variety of habitats, from orchards, parks, and gardens to open woodland and swamps. It is purely nocturnal and is most easily located by its call, a long, quavering whistle which may descend in pitch towards the end. It nests in holes in trees.

Previous pages: the spread wing of a female mallard duck shows the broad, blue speculum edged with white that helps to identify the bird. A diving duck, the splendid hooded merganser (previous pages top inset) is ideally equipped to catch small fish with its long, thin, serrated bill, and the male blue-winged teal (previous pages bottom inset) is unmistakable, with a grey head and a conspicuous white crescent in front of the eye. A wading bird, the least sandpiper (facing page top) is the smallest sandpiper of the region. Small and secretive, the winter wren, (facing page bottom) builds its domed nest in a cavity or hole. It is built by the male and lined by the female. The cedar waxwing (above), so named because of the red, waxy tips to the wing feathers, boasts a fluffy crest and is often seen in large flocks.

Facing page: a pygmy nuthatch at the entrance to its nesting hole, which it has excavated in the dead wood of a tree. As its name suggests, this is the smallest nuthatch found in Canada, and it inhabits ponderosa woodland. The American golden plover (top) is a bird of grassy plains, beaches and tundra. It is often seen in large flocks on migration. In spring, the species can be identified by its black face and underparts, its gold and black back and the striking white stripe that runs from its forehead to its upper breast. The belted kingfisher (above), a large, stocky and heavy-headed bird, is a common sight along rivers and beside ponds, lakes and estuaries. It feeds mainly on fish and can often be seen patiently perched or hovering over the water, before plunging in head first to catch its prey. It normally swallows fish whole.

Its bright red plumage and bill make the male cardinal (facing page top) almost unmistakable. Both sexes have a sizeable conical bill and pointed crests, while the male also has a distinctive black throat patch. This bird has greatly expanded its range northward, and is becoming more frequent in Canada. The slate-coloured or dark-eyed junco (facing page bottom) is greyish overall, but has a white belly, white outer tail feathers and a pinkish bill. It inhabits mixed or coniferous woodland and is found throughout most of the region. In western Canada a subspecies occurs, the Oregon junco, which is very similar, but has a brownish back and buff-coloured sides to the belly. Above: the dark mask of the cedar waxwing is very obvious.

The rare trumpeter swan (top) was once close to extinction, but now, thanks to measures to reintroduce it to former breeding areas, the population is slowly increasing. Named for its call, a deep trumpet-like sound, this is one of the largest swans of the region. Above: a double-crested cormorant displaying at the nest clearly shows the orange-coloured bare skin around the eye and on the throat patch which helps to identify this bird. Famous for its extraordinary migration, the Arctic tern (facing page) probably sees more daylight and travels further than any other animal. After breeding in the north, in almost perpetual daylight, this bird then migrates to spend the winter near the Antarctic, where it again enjoys very long hours of daylight.

The purple sandpiper (top) is found on Canada's eastern seaboard all year round, favouring rocky coasts when on migration, or in winter, when it can frequently be seen on jetties. It prefers to breed on mossy tundra near the coast, but has been seen well inland. The slender and slightly decurved bill has an orange base, a feature which, in addition to the bird's short yellow legs, help to identify it. It is often very tame. The American crow (above) is the largest of the crows, but is smaller than the raven, and its long, black bill is also much less heavy than the raven's. All black and glossy-feathered, it is best identified by its call, the well-known 'caw'. Unmistakable when seen properly, the red-headed woodpecker (facing page) is the only woodpecker with a red head, neck and throat combined with a black necklace and white underparts. It nests in holes in dead trees.

The common redpoll (top left) is identified by its streaked plumage, short stubby bill, red cap and black chin. The breast of the male is usually tinged with pink. In winter this bird is often seen feeding on the seeds of alder and birch. Though similar in size to the peregrine, the prairie falcon (top right) is much paler and browner above, and has a much thinner moustachial stripe. It inhabits dry, open plains country and feeds mainly on birds, though it will also catch rodents. Prairie falcons breed only in the southwest of Canada. The heavy bill of the white-crowned sparrow (above) is ideal for crushing the seeds which form a major part of its diet. Interestingly, the young are fed solely on insects at first. Facing page: a female belted kingfisher, identified by its rusty-coloured flanks and belly band. The male of the species only has the blue breast band.

A long-legged, long-billed bird of marshes and swamps, the American bittern (above) is a common bird, yet, due to its habit of skulking amongst vegetation, it is extremely difficult to observe. The thin black streak on its neck distinguishes it from all other herons, and equally distinctive is its method of avoiding detection. When in danger or alarmed, bitterns adopt an upright stance, their neck, head and bill pointed skywards as they remain completely motionless, a tactic which helps them to blend with their surroundings and thus camouflages them. The familiar black-capped chickadee (facing page top) needs no introduction. Common in most areas of Canada, it is one of the most frequent visitors to the suburban garden if food is provided. Another frequent visitor to gardens in the west is Steller's jay (facing page bottom), which can also be seen on campsites in mixed or coniferous woodland.

Found only in southwest Canada, Lewis' woodpecker (facing page) inhabits open woodland. It differs from most other woodpeckers in having a steady, undulating flight of slow wingbeats, and also in catching most of its insect food in the air. Its red face, grey breast and collar, pink belly and greenish-black head and back give it a distinctive appearance that makes it easy to identify. Top: a floating mat of vegetation provides a nesting site for a pair of Forster's terns. Breeding in central southern

Canada, these birds migrate south in winter. Though they are very similar to Arctic and common terns, their black tipped bill distinguishes them from the Arctic tern, while their grey tail, with its white outer edge, distinguishes them from the common tern. Above: a willet in winter plumage. A long-legged, long-billed wading bird, the willet's summer plumage is browner and heavily mottled.

The bright blue plumage of the male indigo bunting (facing page) makes this bird easily identifiable. The female, on the other hand, is dull brown in colour. Found mainly in southeastern areas of Canada, and inhabiting bushy pastures, woodland edges and clearings, the males like a prominent perch from which to sing. Top: screech owls, whose ear tufts and yellow eyes are good identifying marks. Two different colour forms, or phases, occur in the east of the country and the eastern screech owl, as it is known, can be red or grey. Above: a pair of red-breasted mergansers, where the difference in colour between the sexes is clear. The brighter plumage belongs to the male.

The largest of the godwits, the marbled godwit (facing page top) is brown in colour and mottled, with a black back and barred with black below. Its long bill is usually slightly upturned, though it can be straight, and it breeds in grassy meadows and on the edges of lakes in central Canada. Facing page bottom: a green-backed heron with a successful catch of small fish in its bill. Often it perches amid semi-submerged trees at the water's edge, where it waits for its prey to swim within catching distance. This heron is the second smallest in Canada and its plumage looks more bluish than green on its upper parts. In the breeding season, the yellow legs of the male turn to orange. Found throughout the country, the Canada goose (above) is probably its commonest and best-known goose. Though their markings are all similar, at least ten distinct subspecies occur.

A distinctive feature of the golden eagle (facing page and above left) is the yellow, fleshy cere at the base of the bill. The bill itself is nearly as long as the bird's head. Top: a red-tailed hawk mantling its prey, (left) a fledgling red-tailed hawk, and (above) a goshawk, a bird of forest edges and clearings.

The male evening grosbeak (facing page) is a large, handsome and distinctively-plumaged finch, readily identified by its huge, whitish beak, a yellow forehead that extends back behind and above the eye, yellow underparts and a broad, white patch in an otherwise black wing. Grosbeaks breed throughout southern Canada, and are often seen in noisy flocks uttering a loud, house sparrow-like chirp. Perhaps the commonest and certainly the smallest woodpecker of Canada, the downy woodpecker (top) is the one most likely to visit a garden feeding station. For a woodpecker, it has an extremely short, slender bill, and this, together with its size, distinguishes it from the similarly-marked hairy woodpecker that occupies the same habitat. Above: a splendid male indigo bunting.

The beautifully-marked male harlequin duck (facing page) frequents rocky shorelines in summer, preferring heavy surf to tranquil beaches, while choosing to winter and breed inland on rivers and streams. Surprisingly, despite the conspicuous white flashes and stripes on this duck, the male can look very dark at a distance. The species can sometimes be seen perched on rocks in midstream, but they are rather shy. Top: a pair of American widgeon gaze warily at the photographer. The male is distinguished by his white forehead and cap, and a greenish patch from the eye to the nape, while the drabber female's head and neck has strong, dark streaking. Both sexes have bluish bills. The handsome king eider duck (above) is found mainly in the far north, and is rarely seen inland, spending most of its time around coastal waters, or on lakes and streams near the coast. It nests in the tundra, usually near fresh water.

Top: an adult ring-billed gull, easily identified by the clearly-defined black ring on its bright yellow bill, its pale grey upperparts and white head and underparts. Its wings have black primaries with white spots, and it has yellow eyes and greenish-yellow legs. As with many gulls, full adult plumage is not achieved for three years. Above: a pair of Cassin's auklets, snug in their nesting site, a crevice under stones where only one egg is laid in a nest of plant material. Their plumage is all dark except for a whitish belly and a very small white crescent over the eye. Thick-billed murres (facing page) breed on ledges on rocky coastal cliffs mainly in the northeast . They breed in colonies, often with common murres, and together may number many thousands. The short, thick bill has a narrow, white line at the base.

Wintering in southern Canada, the Lapland longspur (above) breeds in the Arctic tundra. In winter it can be seen in flocks with snow buntings and horned larks, feeding on the shoreline or in fields on grain stubble. Their ground nest, a cup made of grass and lined with hair and feathers, is well hidden by surrounding vegetation. Facing page top: an ovenbird feeding its young, safe in a domed nest among the deep leaf litter on the floor of deciduous woodland. The nest is built by the female, and the bird is usually seen on the ground. A warbler, the ovenbird is distinguished by its brownish-orange crown bordered by blackish stripes and a white eye ring. Cassin's finch (facing page bottom) is found only in a small area of southwest Canada, and is very similar to the purple finch. It is distinguished from the former by its more distinctive capped appearance and its 'kee-up' call.

Facing page: with red combs erect, cocked tail spread and throat puffed out, the male spruce grouse beats his wings in courtship display. The spruce grouse (above) inhabits coniferous forests the width of Canada and, very tame, it will allow the approach of humans. Willow ptarmigan (top), like all other ptarmigan, have very different summer and winter plumages. In winter both sexes are all white, apart from their tails which remain black, which acts as camouflage in the snow. In spring, they begin to change to their summer plumage, and the male is identified by the bright red combs above its eyes and its reddish-brown coloration. Only the wings will remain white. The willow ptarmigan is common on tundra, preferring damp habitats containing willow and alder.

Common on tundra, marsh and in fields, the sandhill crane (facing page) is grey in color, though its plumage may become reddish-brown, when residues in the mud, which are often present on the bill, stain its feathers during preening. It has a distinctive, reddish patch of bare skin on the forehead that aids identification. Cranes are easily distinguished from herons in flight as they fly with necks outstretched, whilst herons fold their necks, and on the ground they are distinctive in that their feathers droop over the rump, forming a 'bustle'. After breeding has finished they usually migrate south in large flocks. The spotted sandpiper (above) is found by rivers, streams, ponds, lakes and marshes, and is common and widespread. On the ground it constantly bobs its tail up and down, while in flight the wings are held stiffly bowed downwards and its wingbeats are very rapid and interspersed with occasional glides.

Though common throughout the country, Canada geese (these pages) seem to prefer to nest in the muskeg region of the Hudson Bay lowlands, a largely waterlogged plain. A pair with the young of that year are inseparable. The female leads the way, followed by the young, with the gander bringing up the rear. The young fly south with their parents in the fall and do not separate from them until they return the following spring to the nesting grounds.

Facing page: fanning its broad, rounded tail, the male ruffed goose tries to attract a female. The black feathers on the side of the neck, forming a ruff, distinguish this bird from all other grouse. It has two colour phases: grey and, in the southwest, a red phase, though the colour variations usually relate only to the tail colour. The extraordinary bill of the red crossbill (top) is specially designed to extract the seeds from pine cones. The male is identified by its reddish plumage, the female being yellowish. Inhabiting coniferous woodlands, these birds are common at times according to the availability of pine cones. Interestingly, young birds do not develop the crossed bill until some ten days after leaving the nest. Above: a female pectoral sandpiper guards its two newly-hatched chicks on the grassy tundra.

A real scavenger, the herring gull (top) is not only found abundantly on the coast, but is also present around inland lakes, rivers, in fields, and especially at garbage dumps. Along the coast it can be seen following fishing boats, picking up offal, or on the shore where it picks up stranded fish and other animals, such as starfish. It is also partial to molluscs, which it drops from the air onto the beach in order to break them open. The semipalmated plover (above) is so named because of the partial webbing between its toes. Breeding on areas of sand, shingle or gravel tundra, usually near water, it makes its nest of a hollow scrape lined with bits of shell and plant material, and usually lays four eggs. Found on the Atlantic coast and in the eastern Arctic, the strikingly-coloured black guillemot (facing page) is unlikely to be confused with any other species.

In the breeding season, the chipping sparrow (facing page top) is identified by its bright chestnut crown, white eyebrow and grey nape and cheek. The female builds the nest with fine grass, usually in a tree in open woodland, and lines it with hair, incubating three to five eggs, and the species is common throughout most of Canada. The black body and bright yellow head and breast of the male yellow-headed blackbird (facing page bottom) makes it unmistakable. Though it favours freshwater marshes and reedy lakes, this bird can also be seen foraging for food in grainfields in southwest Canada. The purple finch (above) is not as purple as the name suggests, but rather rose-red in colour. It breeds across most parts of southern Canada in open woodland, though it can also be seen in suburban gardens.

Facing page: a yellow warbler sitting on its nest, deep in the fork of a tree. Common throughout most of Canada, and probably the country's best-known warbler, this bird favours willow thickets, especially in damp areas, but it is also often found nesting in garden shrubbery. The male Brewer's blackbird (top) is distinguished from the female by its yellow eye and glossy black plumage of purplish sheen, as the female has a brown eye and brown-grey plumage. A bird that often breeds in loose colonies, this blackbird's nest is constructed of twigs and grasses mixed with mud and lined with fine grass or hair. The nest is usually found in a tree or shrub, but it can be on the ground, and is nearly always near water. Above: a hermit thrush feeds its young in a nest set low down in a conifer. This bird is perhaps the finest songster in Canada.

A pale red line above the eye and delicately-patterned brown plumage identify the female willow ptarmigan (previous pages top inset) in summer. Very rare in Canada, the green-tailed towhee (previous pages bottom inset) is identified by its reddish-crown, white throat and olive green plumage. Locally distributed in areas of southern Canada, the pheasant (previous pages) was introduced from Asia. Its spectacularly-bright plumage and long tail make the male impossible to confuse with any other species in Canada. Facing page: a long-eared owl devouring a small rodent. Here the characteristic long ears are flattened. This is a strictly nocturnal bird, common in woods near open country. Top: a rough-legged hawk scavenging on an animal carcass. These hawks often hover whilst hunting and usually feed on rodents. Above: a barred owl emerging from its nest site in a hollow tree.

These pages: a wealth of wildfowl. The green-winged teal (left), Canada's smallest duck, measures 10.5 inches (27 cm.) in length. Above left: the male greater scaup, (top) American coots displaying, and (above) the common loon, which returns to its breeding grounds soon after the winter ice breaks up. Facing page: (top) a wood duck, and (bottom) a mallard hen guarding her resting ducklings.

Facing page: a double-crested cormorant towering over its chick has already lost the feature for which it is named. Early in the spring the adult has a tuft of feathers either side of the head, whitish in colour in western cormorants and black in eastern, but these are quickly lost once breeding commences. The nestling has a pink, rather than a yellow, throat patch. Top: standing on its floating nest of dead plant material, a Franklin's gull prepares to incubate its two eggs. A gull of the prairies, large numbers of these birds nest together in colonies. Breeding in the Arctic, the snow goose (above) is a common and an especially abundant migrant to parts of eastern Canada, where many thousands can be seen feeding on the marshes. Two colour phases occur in this bird, the white phase and the 'blue' phase, which has a brown back.

Wintering in South America, the lesser yellowlegs (above) is a common bird that migrates to Canada to breed. Two species of yellowlegs occur, the lesser and the greater. As its name implies, the lesser is the smaller of the two, and it also has a thinner, shorter, straight bill when compared with that of the greater. The two species are often seen together on migration, and long, bright yellow legs are common to both. The lesser yellowlegs breeds in open woodlands and tundra near ponds and lakes. With similar markings and ear tufts to the long-eared owl, the great-horned owl (facing page) is much larger. Several colour forms occur in this species, ranging from dark brown through reddish-brown to extremely pale, greyish-brown plumages. As with all owls, these birds swallow the whole of their prey, later to cough up pellets of bone, fur, feathers and other indigestible matter.

The hawk owl (facing page) has a long tail, which gives it a falcon-like appearance, especially in flight. Its other distinguishing features are its heavily-barred underparts and the black border of its pale facial disk. Hunting in daylight, it is often seen prominently perched on a tree top, where it has the curious habit of flicking its tail up and then lowering it slowly. Its flight is rapid, interspersed with glides, and it also hovers. This owl inhabits the muskegs and coniferous and deciduous woodland of northern

Canada, and is usually very tame. The osprey (above) is identified by its dark brown upperpart, white underparts and white head with a dark stripe through the eye. Here the bird is almost certainly male, as females tend to have some dark streaking on the breast, forming a necklace. The osprey's deeply-hooked bill is ideal for tearing at its prey, which encompasses both sea and freshwater fish.

Very similar to the sharp-shinned hawk, but larger, Cooper's hawk (above) is identified when fully mature by the reddish barring on its underparts and its long, rounded tail. Immature birds have pale underparts with fine, dark streaking. An uncommon hawk, it inhabits woodland across the southernmost parts of Canada. Occupying a similar habitat to that of Cooper's hawk, the adult goshawk (facing page top) has greyish barring on its underparts and a white line above the eye, which helps to differentiate between the two birds. The goshawk's nest is constructed almost entirely by the male, and the hawk breeds in woodlands throughout most of central and southern Canada. Most adult red-tailed hawks (facing page bottom) are identified by their broad, reddish tails, which are darker red above than below. However, there are several different colour forms of this hawk in Canada, in some of which the red is very pale, or even non-existent. The bird is common in open country.

The golden eagle (facing page) is distinguished by its strong, hooked beak, overall brown plumage and feathered legs. Its favourite hunting grounds are foothills with grassy pastures where prey such as the yellow-bellied marmot live. Remaining pictures: an eagle with its marmot prey.

Top: the adult blue jay tends to its young in their tree nest. Colourful birds, with blue upperparts and white underparts, these jays are easily identified by the white in their wings and tail, which distinguish them from the otherwise similar Steller's jay. Noisy and inquisitive, the blue jay can be found in woodlands, parks and suburban gardens. The lazuli bunting (above) is found in bushy scrub and open woodland, especially near water, throughout southwestern Canada. Facing page: an eastern kingbird standing over its young. Breeding in much of western and southern Canada, these birds nest on tree branches or posts, usually near or over water. Three to four eggs are laid in a deep, cup-shaped nest that is lined with hair.

A long, thin, slightly upturned bill identifies the American avocet (above). The plumage of this bird is mainly black and white, with a rust-coloured head and neck. The long, blue legs facilitate wading in shallow water, necessary in the search for food, which is obtained by sweeping the bill from side to side in the water. The avocet breeds in colonies on the shores of lakes or on islands in central southern Canada. A great blue heron (facing page top) is the largest heron to be found in Canada, and it is also the most numerous. It has a dramatic method of hunting. Standing motionless in the water, or slowly stalking its prey – mainly fishes or amphibians – the heron will suddenly lunge forward and grasp its unfortunate victim in its bill. Facing page bottom: the black oystercatcher. Inhabiting rocky shores, and breeding only on the extreme west coast of Canada, this oystercatcher is immediately recognisable from its all-black plumage, long red bill and distinctive pink legs.

Previous pages: a black oystercatcher, its red eye ring clearly visible, grasping a limpet. Previous pages inset: a small group of ruddy turnstones gathered on a rock. These birds gained their name from their characteristic habit of flipping stones over in search of food. They breed in the Arctic, and are common along Canadian coasts, though rare inland. Facing page top: a red-breasted nuthatch entering its nest hole with food for its young. This is the only Canadian nuthatch with a white stripe. The male red-shafted flicker (facing page bottom), a woodpecker, can be identified by its red 'moustache', as the female lacks this feature. A member of the flycatcher species, the eastern kingbird (above) is most often seen perched in the open on a tree or post, where it waits to fly out and catch passing insects. These birds are identified by their dark, almost black, upperparts, white underparts and the white terminal band on their tail.

The black oystercatcher (left) is a bird which breeds on the rocky Pacific coast, while the chukar partridge (above left) is an Asian bird introduced to Canada. Above: a ptarmigan in summer dress, and (top) a Californian quail. Facing page: (top) a wild turkey in the snow, and (bottom) a ringneck pheasant.

Facing page top: the female rufous hummingbird, and (top) the male of the species. These hummingbirds can be found breeding in parts of western Canada, while the ruby-throated hummingbird (facing page bottom) breeds across much of southern Canada, except in the far west. The calliope hummingbird (above) is not only the smallest Canadian hummingbird, it is also the smallest North American bird. Its nest is minute, less than an inch high, and is bound together with spider's webs. These three hummingbirds belong to a group found only in the New World and, feeding on nectar or small insects found in flowers, they are capable of hovering in front or under blooms while they feed. So-named after the noise of their rapidly-beating wings, these small and seemingly-delicate birds are capable of migrating long distances south to warmer climes in winter.

The European mute swan (top) is an introduced species which has become wild in a few parts of Canada. The whistling swan (above), a magnificent, all-white bird, breeds in the Canadian low Arctic. Left: a coot feeding its young, and (above left) a red-winged blackbird and swan. Snow geese (facing page top) can be seen in large numbers in the fall at Cap Tourmente, east of Quebec City. Facing page bottom: a mallard hen with nestlings.

Facing page: a female yellow-shafted flicker feeds its young at the entrance to its nest hole in a dead tree. The red patch on the nape of the neck helps to identify this bird; the males have a black 'moustache', though otherwise the sexes are very similar in plumage. This particular woodpecker can often be seen on the ground, where it feeds on ants. Top: mouths agape for food, nestling western meadowlarks show off their bright red gapes.

Nesting on the ground in grassy fields, the female builds the domed nest and it alone incubates the eggs, though the male helps to feed the offspring. The song sparrow (above) also builds its nest on the ground, breeding in bushy thickets and shrubbery close to ponds and streams. The adults are highly variable in size and plumage, but all show a greyish line above the eye.

The adult male Hudsonian godwit (top) is mainly a migrant to Canada. Although it does nest in parts of the country, much of its breeding range is unknown. In flight its white wing stripes, black tail and white rump are striking, and it is also identified by its slightly upcurved bill. Equally unmistakable, American avocets (above) are found on the shores of marshes and lakes. The male American goldfinch (facing page) is commonly known as the 'wild canary'. Its bright yellow plumage is strikingly offset by a black cap, wings and tail. The male's wings have white bars and its rump is also white, while the female is much duller and lacks the black cap. This finch is found on roadsides, in orchards and in weedy fields, and it is especially fond of thistle seeds, which gives it yet another name: the 'thistle bird'.

Tame enough to allow close approach, the hawk owl (facing page top) is one of the few owls that remain active in the daytime. The peculiar lobed toes of the American coot (facing page bottom) help to distinguish this bird from similiar gallinules, and also help it to swim more effectively. An American coot is easy to identify by its slate-coloured body and black head with red eye, its heavy, white bill with a dark band near the tip, the reddish shield on its forehead, and white outer feathers on its undertail. Top: a female American woodcock and its chick sit tight on the nest, perfectly camouflaged amongst the dead leaves of the forest floor. A bright reddish-orange rump and tail identify the fox sparrow (above) in eastern Canada. Their plumage is highly variable, however, and in the west these birds are much darker and drabber.

Once known as the pigeon hawk, the merlin (previous pages) is a very small and dashing falcon. In flight it shows considerable bursts of speed as it chases its prey, which consists of small birds. Its strongly-barred tail and pointed wings help to identify this bird. Previous pages inset: a gyrfalcon with its prey. A much bigger bird than the merlin, this falcon feeds mainly on large birds, such as ptarmigan, and rodents, and it occurs in three colour phases: a grey phase, a dark phase which is brown, and a white phase, which is the commonest in the eastern high Arctic. Nesting in large colonies on cliffs, common murres (above) are distinguished from other alcids by their white sides and long, slender bill. Facing page: (top) red-breasted mergansers and (bottom) a hooded merganser. Both these species of diving duck have crests, the most prominent belonging to the male hooded merganser.

Facing page: (top) a female belted kingfisher eyes the water below, waiting for a fish to swim past, and (bottom) an Arctic loon prepares to incubate its two eggs nestling in a shallow heap of vegetation. Both sexes of this loon incubate the eggs, which hatch after 28 or 29 days. The loon's nest is never very far from water, as it finds great difficulty in walking on land. A beautiful bird, the feathers on the neck of the adult are so fine and dense as to appear like velvet. 'Kra-a-a' is the call of Clark's nutcracker (top). Its all-grey body contrasts with its black wings and tail, while the outer tail feathers and a small wing patch are white. This nutcracker inhabits high, coniferous forests, descending in winter, when it often scavenges at campsites. Above: a long-eared owl, readily identified by its ear tufts.

The osprey (left and facing page bottom) is a spectacular bird of prey that builds its nest in tall trees near water. It can be identified at long distances by the characteristic crook in its long wings. The American avocet (top and facing page top) utters an alarm-like 'kleep' when disturbed. Its preferred haibitat is the shallow lakes and sloughs of the southern prairie provinces. The herring gull (above) is a universal scavenger.

A black head, a white line over the eye, and reddish underparts identify the red-breasted nuthatch (facing page top). The nuthatch favours coniferous forest, and has the extraordinary ability to walk both up and down the trunks of trees whilst searching for food. Its nest hole is excavated in a dead tree or stump and four to nine eggs are laid. They are found, in suitable habitat, right across Canada, and migrate irregularly, often in alternate years. Facing page bottom: a male yellow warbler feeding its nestlings. Rusty-red streaking on the underparts help to identify this bird, and its nest is usually in a fork of twigs in a shrub or a tree and is made of fine grasses, lined with cotton and plant down. The young leave the nest nine to twelve days after hatching. Above: the brightly-colored male purple finch, the size of a house sparrow.

The female evening grosbeak (top) is identified by its heavy, conical bill, greyish plumage with a greenish-yellow nape, and much white on its wings and tail. In the breeding season these birds inhabit mixed or coniferous woodland, but in winter they can easily be attracted to garden feeding stations by the provision of sunflower seeds. They are most often seen in flocks. Wilson's snipe (above) is also known as the common snipe, and is usually seen perching in the open on its breeding ground. The males' spring display flight includes a dive with a fanned tail that, in vibrating air through the feathers, produces a characteristic 'who-who-who' sound. The distinctive head pattern of the adult lark sparrow (facing page top) is an aid to accurate identification. Both sexes of the mourning dove (facing page bottom) incubate the eggs, the male during the day, and the female at night.

Facing page: a resplendent male yellow-headed blackbird perches on a bullrush at the edge of a marsh. The white area on the wing of the male forms a noticeable patch in flight; females lack this patch and their plumage is dusky brown instead of black, their head and breast usually being buffish yellow. Large and plump, with a stubby bill, the pine grosbeak (top) is usually very tame. Its reddish plumage and double wing bars help to identify the male, while the female is greyish overall, with olive on the head and rump, though it too has the distinctive double wing bars. These are birds of the coniferous forests in summer, and can be found in deciduous woodland, apple orchards and suburban shade trees in winter. The conspicuous crest of the blue jay (above) helps to identify this bird, a colourful Canadian resident throughout the year.

Above: a mountain bluebird at its nest hole, (top) a killdeer on its nest, (top right) a yellow-bellied sapsucker with its beak full of insects, and (right) a long-billed curlew chick. Facing page: (top left) a caliope hummingbird, (top right) Bewick's wren, (bottom right) a tree swallow, and (bottom left) a yellow-headed blackbird.

A rich, fruity, bubbling song distinguishes the western meadowlark (facing page) from its look-alike, the eastern meadowlark, both of which occur in Canada. Its main plumage features in summer are a yellow throat, breast and belly, a black, V-shaped necklace on the throat, black streaking on the flanks, and a striped head. The call is very distinctive, a throaty 'chuck'. Found in open, grassy stubble fields in autumn, this bird prefers drier habitats than the eastern meadowlark. Top: a winter-plumaged willow ptarmigan, well camouflaged against the snow. This camouflage is very important, as ptarmigan is often preyed upon by birds, such as the gyrfalcon, which relies on its sense of sight to find its prey. Above: part of a flock of migrating Canada geese rest in a grassy field before continuing their journey. The characteristic honking flight call is well-known to all Canadians.

Above: a blue jay, its large, white-tipped tail feathers clearly visible. This species has a very varied diet, including insects, fruit, acorns, and also the eggs and nestlings of other birds, though is it doubtful whether this has any significant impact upon the population of the birds that form its prey. Facing page top: the nest of a Brewer's sparrow, built low in a small shrub. A bird of the scrub and sagebush, this sparrow builds its nest of dry grass and lines it with fine grass and hair. This is one of the duller-coloured sparrows, being plain grey below and streaked on its upperparts, but usually two very faint wing bars can be seen. Facing page bottom: a prairie falcon on the lookout for prey.

Facing page: a violet-green swallow bracing its tail against a tree trunk for support, rather like a treecreeper. Found in western Canada, the violet-green swallow nests in old woodpecker holes in trees, in crevices in cliffs, or in nestboxes. Identified by its glossy, violet-green upperparts and white cheeks, these birds are seen catching their insect prey over woodland, water and fields. Conspicuous yellow and white wing bars identify the western tanager (top). The upper wing bar is bright yellow, the thinner, lower bar whitish, and the males's bright red head contrasts with its startling yellow neck and underparts. This tanager is found in mixed or coniferous woodland in western Canada. Above: a rufous hummingbird hovers to sip nectar from a flower. It can be identified as a female by the spots on its throat.

Clark's nutcracker (top) lives in open conifer woods in the west of Canada. Above: pigeons, and (above right) the emperor goose, a rare winter visitor to the coast of British Columbia. The other common name for the spruce grouse (right) is 'fool hen' because its tameness often allows it to be killed with a stick or a stone. It prefers the forest edges and blueberry barrens. The wild turkey (facing page) was once extinct in Canada, but attempts have now been made to reintroduce it into hardwood forests.

The powerful golden eagle (top) makes its home in mountainous country, while the prairie falcon (right) is found in the dry, open country of the west, as is Swainson's hawk (facing page top), which hunts mainly prairie dogs and gophers, as well as large insects such as grasshoppers. The red-tailed hawk (top right) is a lazy hunter that soars high above the ground, and the bald eagle (facing page bottom) eats fish and also takes sick ducks and game birds. Above: marsh hawk eggs and nestlings.

Despite its enormous beak, the bald eagle (these pages) is more of a scavenger than an active hunter. Its food consists mainly of dead fish washed up on the coast, or by lakes and rivers, and it has recently declined in numbers. Its nest, built in a tall tree, may become huge, as it is often returned to and enlarged year after year.

Top: a male greater prairie chicken performs its courtship display. With tail cocked and crest erect, it bows and inflates its orange neck sacs behind its long, fanned, neck feathers. During this display the male makes a deep, hollow-sounding 'oo-loo-woo' call, known as booming, in front of the females on a defined courtship ground. The ruffed grouse (above) inhabits mixed woodland, especially the clearings within woods, and can be found in a wide area west to east across Canada. Breeding in eastern Canada, the red-shouldered hawk (facing page) is so named after the reddish patch of feathers on its 'shoulder'. Its darkish wings have strong, white barring, and the blackish tail has narrow, white bands, while its whitish underparts are closely barred with reddish-orange. This hawk inhabits mixed woodland, and is often seen soaring in circles, or else perching whilst watching for its prey of small birds, frogs, reptiles and rodents.

Below: an Arctic tern alights beside its young chick on a pebble-strewn, sandy shore. One to four eggs are usually laid and the immature gull is distinguished from the adult by its black bill. Bottom: a killdeer lowers itself over its four eggs in a shallow scrape. This bird will feign personal injury to distract intruders away from its nest, and is identified by a double black breast band. Facing page top: a flock of whimbrel march along a mudflat at sunset. Whimbrel have a short, gentle-sounding whistle that is rapidly repeated six to seven times, and they are common in marshes, mudflats and shorelines. By contrast, the whooping crane (facing page bottom) is dangerously close to extinction today. So named for its ringing, vibrant call, this elegant and dignified bird is carefully protected now.

Facing page top: a green-backed heron resting on a rock. This heron is seen along wooded streams or on small ponds more commonly than other herons, and often appears to be all dark at a distance. Facing page bottom: a winter-plumaged flock of red knot resting on a shoreline during migration. In the spring, their grey backs and robin-like breasts are distinctive, and they are common on sandy shores, mudflats and rocks. The long-billed curlew (above) is the largest shore bird in Canada, and is easily distinguished by its slender, extremely long, down-curved bill and cinnamon upperparts. During the breeding season, it nests in meadows and pastures, and the sexes are similar in appearance.

Clark's nutcracker (top and facing page) feeds on nuts and conifer seeds, and is found among conifers near the timberline, though it can be seen at lower levels. Above: a male mountain bluebird at its nest in an abandoned woodpecker hole, (above right) the grey jay of the northern forests, and (right) Steller's jay, which lives in western Canada.

Facing page: a saw-whet owl and its prey. This eight-inch (20cm) long bird prefers to nest in moist, mixed forest. The great horned owl (top and right) is Canada's largest and takes prey such as hares. Above: a male and (above right) a female snowy owl, members of a species that breeds in the Arctic tundra.

Above: a long-billed curlew, a breeding bird of the grasslands of southwest Canada. The great blue heron (remaining pictures), Canada's largest heron, is a statuesque bird that gives a harsh alarm call of four hoarse squawks.

A rose-breasted grosbeak (facing page) is easily identified by its distinctive black head and back, white wing bars, massive bill, and the bright red patch on its breast. Common in deciduous woodland, in flight its red wing linings and the white patches on its wings show from below. The barn swallow (top) could be mistaken for the cliff swallow, as the two species share bright cinnamon underparts and a red forehead and throat. However, the long streamers of its deeply-forked tail conclusively identify the barn swallow. It is a strong and elegant flier, common near farms, and nests in farm buildings, under bridges and in caves. Often found in flocks in winter, the pine grosbeak (above) has the strong, heavy bill typical of a seed-eater, and the males are a beautiful rose red color, with white wing bars contrasting against dark wings. It is a species found in Canada throughout the year. Overleaf: singing to proclaim his territory, the male red-winged blackbird shows off his yellow-bordered, bright red wing patches.

159